EVE EATS EVERYTHING
AN ADVENTURE WITH THE VOWEL E

by Brandon Terrell
illustrated by Daniela Massironi

GRASSHOPPER

Tools for Parents & Teachers

Grasshopper Books enhance imagination and introduce the earliest readers to fiction with fun storylines and illustrations. The easy-to-read text supports early reading experiences with repetitive sentence patterns and sight words.

Before Reading

- Look at the cover illustration. What do readers see? What do they think the book will be about?

- Look at the picture glossary together. Sound out the words. Ask readers to identify the first letter of each vocabulary word.

Read the Book

- "Walk" through the book, reading to or along with the reader. Point to the illustrations as you read.

After Reading

- Review the picture glossary again. Ask readers to locate the words in the text.

- Ask the reader: What does a short 'e' sound like? What does a long 'e' sound like? Which words did you see in the book with these sounds? What other words do you know that have these sounds?

Grasshopper Books are published by Jump!
5357 Penn Avenue South
Minneapolis, MN 55419
www.jumplibrary.com

Library of Congress Cataloging-in-Publication Data

Names: Terrell, Brandon, 1978-2021 author.
Massironi, Daniela, illustrator.
Title: Eve eats everything : an adventure with the vowel e / by Brandon Terrell; illustrated by Daniela Massironi.
Description: Minneapolis, MN: Jump!, Inc., [2022]
Series: Vowel adventures
Includes reading tips and supplementary back matter.
Audience: Ages 5-7.
Identifiers: LCCN 2021000077 (print)
LCCN 2021000078 (ebook)
ISBN 9781636902401 (hardcover)
ISBN 9781636902418 (paperback)
ISBN 9781636902425 (ebook)
Subjects: LCSH: Readers (Primary)
Grocery shopping–Juvenile fiction.
Classification: LCC PE1119.2 .T474 2022 (print)
LCC PE1119.2 (ebook)
DDC 428.6/2–dc23
LC record available at https://lccn.loc.gov/2021000077
LC ebook record available at https://lccn.loc.gov/2021000078

Editor: Eliza Leahy
Direction and Layout: Anna Peterson
Illustrator: Daniela Massironi

Printed in the United States of America at Corporate Graphics in North Mankato, Minnesota.

Brandon M. Terrell (B.1978-D.2021) was a talented storyteller, authoring more than 100 books for children. He was a passionate reader, Star Wars enthusiast, amazing father, and devoted husband. This book is dedicated in his memory. Happy reading!

Table of Contents

Let's Eat!

The grocery store opens. Eve and her stepdad, Ed, enter.

"My belly is empty!" Eve whines.

"Let's get burgers.
We'll eat ten each!"

5

Ed sees veggies.

"Let's see. Red and green peppers? Leeks? Peas, perhaps?" he asks.

"Yes, please!" Eve says.

Peas

Peas

7

Eve sees peaches.

"These are nice. See, Ed?" she asks.

"Let's select seven," Ed says.

"Sweet!" says Eve.

"Cheese!" Eve yells. "I love brie!"

"I agree. We'll get three wheels." Ed says.

"We need eggs. Is eight dozen enough?" Eve asks.

"Yes! Excellent!" Ed says.

Eve sees sweets.

"Yes!" she says. "I really enjoy sweets."

Ed peers at the cart.

"Eek! We have everything."

Eve smiles. "Yes. Let's eat!"

Let's Review Vowel E!

Point to the words with the short 'e' sound you saw in the book.
Point to the words with the long 'e' sound.

peppers   **sweets**   **eggs**   **belly**   **peaches**   **brie**

Picture Glossary

dozen
A group of twelve.

leeks
Vegetables with slender white bulbs and green leaves.

peers
Looks closely at something.

select
To choose something carefully.